47 Techniques ways to earn $2000 monthly online

Practical Handbook for Anyone Who Wants to Work from Home and Earn More Money.

KENDRICK BANKS

Table of contents

Chapter 1: Introduction

In the modern age, the internet has opened up a world of opportunities, and one of the most enticing prospects it offers is the ability to make money online. The possibilities are boundless, and this guide, titled "How to Make $2,000 a Month Online: 47 Ways to Make Money Online," aims to be your comprehensive compass through this digital landscape. We will navigate the avenues where you can harness the power of the internet to transform your financial aspirations into reality.

The allure of making money online has grown exponentially in recent years. It's not just a source of extra income; for many, it has evolved into a primary means of financial support, if not a full-time career. The digital era has dismantled traditional workplace boundaries, offering an array of possibilities that empower individuals to take control of their financial destinies. Whether you're a digital native or someone who's recently embraced the online world, the potential to earn a living, or even achieve substantial wealth, is at your fingertips.

This guide embarks on a journey of exploration, revealing the manifold ways to make money online. Its core goal is to inform, inspire, and equip you with the knowledge and strategies required to generate income in the digital domain. As we progress through the chapters, you'll discover various avenues, each with its unique strengths and challenges. We'll traverse the terrain of freelancing, e-commerce, passive income streams, online services, skill-based income, and even investment opportunities, opening doors to a world of financial possibilities.

The essence of this guide is not just to provide information but also to serve as a catalyst for your financial success. While there's no guarantee of immediate riches, the strategies and insights you'll gather here will set you on the path to achieving your financial goals. The journey begins by understanding that making money online is more than just a desire—it's a commitment. It's a journey that requires dedication, perseverance, and adaptability to the ever-changing digital landscape.

As we delve deeper into the various income-generating opportunities, keep in mind that your success story is unique. You may be a skilled writer, a creative artist, a tech-savvy entrepreneur, or a specialist in a particular field. The beauty of this guide is that it caters to a diverse audience, offering something for everyone, regardless of your background or interests. The internet's versatility means there's a place for all kinds of talents and skills to thrive, and your path to financial prosperity is just a few pages away.

So, fasten your seatbelt, for the journey ahead is both thrilling and full of promise. We'll help you sharpen your skills and expand your horizons, opening doors to income streams you might not have considered. Whether you're in pursuit of a side hustle, a part-time gig, or the dream of quitting your nine-to-five grind, the digital world offers opportunities aplenty. This guide is your gateway to those opportunities, and our goal is to empower you with the knowledge you need to seize them.

Now, let's embark on this expedition into the realm of making money online. Our destination: financial independence. Your co-pilot: this guide. The possibilities are boundless, and the journey is about to begin. Welcome aboard!

ethereum
ZCASH
CASH
DIGITAL CURRENCY · MONERO · SEC

Chapter 2: Freelancing Opportunities

Freelancing has become a cornerstone of the modern workforce. In an era where traditional employment structures are evolving, freelancing offers flexibility and opportunities for individuals to craft their own careers. In this chapter, we will explore various freelancing opportunities, highlighting key sectors and sharing insights on how to succeed in this dynamic field.

Writing and Content Creation

Writing and content creation have emerged as one of the most popular freelancing options in the digital age. The demand for high-quality content is insatiable, driven by the proliferation of online platforms, blogs, social media, and e-commerce websites. Businesses and individuals alike require compelling content to engage their audience and drive their online presence. If you have a flair for words and the ability to convey ideas effectively, freelance writing and content creation can be a lucrative path.

Exploring Freelance Writing and Content Creation

1. **Content Writing**: Content writers produce articles, blog posts, and web copy. They need to be versatile in their writing style and adapt to different topics and industries.

2. **Copywriting**: Copywriters specialize in creating persuasive and compelling text for advertising and marketing materials. They play a crucial role in crafting messages that drive sales.

3. **Technical Writing**: Technical writers excel in producing clear and concise documentation, often related to complex subjects like software, engineering, or medical information.

4. **Blogging**: If you have expertise in a specific field or a passion for storytelling, you can start your blog. Successful bloggers can monetize their content through advertising, sponsored posts, and affiliate marketing.

5. **Ghostwriting**: Ghostwriters are hired to write books, articles, or content on behalf of someone else. This is a common practice in the publishing industry, where celebrities and experts often need assistance to turn their ideas into written works.

Building Your Freelance Writing Career

- **Portfolio Development**: As a freelance writer or content creator, your portfolio is your calling card. It's essential to have a collection of your best work to showcase your skills and style to potential clients. You can create a personal blog or website to display your work.

- **Networking:** Joining online communities and forums for writers can be beneficial. Networking with other freelancers and potential clients can lead to job opportunities and collaborations.

- **Content Mills vs. Private Clients**: Content mills are platforms where you can find writing gigs, but they often pay lower rates. Working with private clients can be more lucrative in the long run. Building relationships with businesses and agencies can lead to ongoing work.

- **Pricing Your Services**: Setting your rates can be challenging. Consider your experience, the complexity of the work, and industry standards. Over time, you can increase your rates as you gain experience and a strong reputation.

- **Time Management:** Freelancers need excellent time management skills. You'll be juggling multiple projects and deadlines. Using tools like calendars and project management software can help you stay organized.

Graphic Design and Digital Art

Visual communication is at the heart of modern media. From branding and marketing to web design and user experience, the demand for talented graphic designers and digital artists is immense. If you have a knack for creativity, a strong visual sense, and proficiency with design software, a freelance career in graphic design could be your calling.

Exploring Graphic Design and Digital Art Freelancing

1. **Logo Design:** Creating unique and memorable logos for businesses is a sought-after skill. Logos are the face of a brand, and they play a crucial role in brand identity.

2. **Web Design:** Web designers are responsible for the visual aspects of websites, ensuring they are user-friendly and visually appealing. This field is continually evolving with the latest design trends and technologies.

3. **Illustration:** Digital illustrators create images, graphics, and artwork for various purposes, such as book covers, magazines, advertisements, and web content.

4. **UI/UX Design:** User interface (UI) and user experience (UX) designers focus on creating interfaces that are intuitive and user-friendly. They play a critical role in app and website design.

5. **Print Design:** Print designers work on projects like brochures, flyers, posters, and business cards. Despite the digital age, print materials are still essential for marketing and branding.

Building Your Graphic Design and Digital Art Freelance Career

- **Create a Striking Portfolio:** Much like writers, graphic designers and digital artists should have a portfolio showcasing their best work. Ensure it reflects your style and versatility.

- **Stay Updated:** Design trends change frequently. It's essential to stay up to date with the latest software and design techniques. Continuous learning and professional development are crucial.

- **Collaborate and Seek Feedback:** Collaboration with clients and fellow designers can provide valuable insights and improve your skills. Don't hesitate to seek feedback to enhance your work.

- **Market Your Services**: Building an online presence through social media and professional networking platforms like LinkedIn can help potential clients discover your services.

- **Leverage Online Marketplaces:** Websites like Behance and Dribbble allow you to showcase your work and connect with potential clients. They serve as platforms for discovery by businesses seeking design talent.

<u>Web Development and Design</u>

In today's digital age, an online presence is a prerequisite for businesses and individuals alike. Web developers and designers play a pivotal role in creating and maintaining websites that are both functional and visually appealing. This field offers numerous opportunities for those with coding and design skills.

Exploring Web Development and Design Freelancing

1. **Front-End Development:** Front-end developers focus on the visible aspects of websites, such as layout, design, and

user interface. They are those that work with technologies like HTML, CSS, and JavaScript.

2. **Back-End Development:** Back-end developers manage the server-side of websites, handling databases, servers, and application logic. They often work with languages like Python, PHP, and Ruby.

3. **Full-Stack Development:** Full-stack developers excel in both front-end and back-end development, possessing a holistic grasp of the entire web development workflow.

4. **Web Design:** Web designers specialize in creating the visual aspects of websites, including layouts, graphics, and user experience. They often work closely with front-end developers to bring designs to life.

5. **E-commerce Development:** E-commerce developers focus on creating and maintaining online stores. They work with platforms like WooCommerce, Shopify, and Magento to enable online sales.

Building Your Web Development and Design Freelance Career

- **Skills Development:** Stay current with programming languages, frameworks, and design tools. Continuous learning is essential to remain competitive in this rapidly evolving field.

- **Portfolio Showcasing:** Your portfolio should highlight your best projects and demonstrate your skills. It's a critical tool for attracting clients.

- **Responsive Design:** With the growing use of mobile devices, understanding responsive web design is crucial. Websites must be accessible and look good on various screen sizes.

- **Establishing Client Connections:** Cultivating robust client connections has the potential to result in recurring transactions and word-of-mouth recommendations. Communication skills are vital in understanding client needs and delivering solutions.

- **Freelance Platforms:** Utilize freelancing platforms like Upwork, Freelancer, and Toptal to find clients and projects. These platforms offer a vast marketplace for web development and design services.

Virtual Assistance

The role of a virtual assistant has gained prominence as businesses and entrepreneurs seek to streamline their operations and reduce overhead costs. Virtual assistants provide administrative support and manage tasks remotely, offering a flexible work arrangement for both clients and freelancers.

Exploring Virtual Assistance Freelancing

1. **Administrative Support**: Virtual assistants handle tasks such as email management, scheduling, data entry, and document preparation.

2. **Customer Service**: Some virtual assistants specialize in providing customer support through email, chat, or phone. They address customer inquiries and concerns.

3. Social Media Management: Managing social media accounts, including content creation, posting schedules, and engagement, is a significant aspect of virtual assistance.

4. **Research and Data Analysis**: Virtual assistants may conduct research, gather data, and generate reports for clients.

5. **E-commerce Support**: E-commerce businesses often require virtual assistants to manage product listings, monitor inventory, and handle customer orders.

Building Your Virtual Assistance Freelance Career

- **Skill Set**: Develop skills in areas like time management, communication, and proficiency in tools such as Microsoft Office, project management software, and social media platforms.

- **Professionalism**: Building a reputation for reliability and professionalism is essential. Meeting established timeframes and surpassing client anticipations will result in recurrent patronage.

- **Niche Specialization**: Consider specializing in a niche, such as real estate or healthcare, where specific industry knowledge can be an asset.

- **Freelance Platforms**: Websites like Upwork, Fiverr, and Virtual Assistant Forums are valuable resources for finding virtual assistant gigs.

- **Marketing and Networking**: Utilize social media and professional networks like LinkedIn to market your services and connect with potential clients.

Online Tutoring and Teaching

The field of education has seen a significant transformation with the rise of online tutoring and teaching. This sector offers opportunities for educators and subject matter experts to share their knowledge with a global audience.

Exploring Online Tutoring and Teaching Freelancing

1. **Language Instruction**: Teaching languages, such as English, Spanish, or Mandarin, is a popular option. There's a constant demand for language instructors.

2. **Academic Subjects**: Online tutoring extends to various academic subjects, from mathematics and science to history and literature. Tutors can assist students at various levels.

3. **Test Preparation**: Help students prepare for standardized tests like the SAT, ACT, GRE, or GMAT. Test preparation is a niche that can be highly profitable.

4. **Music and Art Instruction:** If you're a musician or artist, you can offer lessons online. Platforms like Udemy and Skillshare are excellent for creating and selling courses.

5. **Professional Skills:** Share your expertise in fields like programming, graphic design, or digital marketing. Many learners are eager to acquire these skills.

Building Your Online Tutoring and Teaching Freelance Career

- **Teaching Certification:** Depending on the subject and platform, having teaching certification or relevant qualifications can enhance your credibility.

- **Content Creation:** If you create your courses, ensure they are well-structured and engaging. High-quality content can lead to positive reviews and more students.

- **Interactive Methods:** Engage students through interactive teaching methods, such as live webinars, quizzes, and discussions. Encourage participation and learning.

- **Feedback and Improvement:** Collect and act on feedback from students. Continuous improvement of your teaching methods and content is key to success.

- **Promotion:** Promote your courses or tutoring services through your website, social media, and online teaching platforms. Building a personal brand can attract more students.

Chapter 3: E-commerce and Online Selling

The digital revolution has not only changed the way we communicate and work but also the way we shop and do business. E-commerce, the practice of buying and selling products or services online, has experienced explosive growth in recent years. This chapter delves into various e-commerce and online selling strategies that can help you make money online.

Starting an Online Store

Starting your online store is an exciting venture that allows you to showcase and sell products or services directly to customers. E-commerce has democratized retail, enabling individuals and small businesses to reach a global audience.

Exploring Starting an Online Store

1. Choosing a Niche: The first step in starting an online store is selecting a niche. Consider your interests, expertise, and market demand. A well-defined niche can set your store apart.

2. **E-commerce Platforms:** Choose an e-commerce platform to build and manage your online store. Popular platforms include Shopify, WooCommerce, BigCommerce, and Wix. Each of them has its own features and its pricing.

3. **Product Selection:** Decide whether you'll sell physical products, digital goods, or a combination of both. Source or create your products, ensuring they align with your niche and target audience.

4. **Website Design:** Create an attractive and user-friendly website. The design should reflect your brand and be optimized for mobile devices. High-quality images and detailed product descriptions are essential.

5. **Payment and Shipping:** Set up secure payment options and establish shipping processes. Consider factors like shipping costs, delivery times, and international shipping for a global reach.

6. **Marketing and SEO:** Develop a marketing strategy that includes search engine optimization (SEO), social media marketing, email campaigns, and advertising. Effective marketing drives traffic to your site and boosts sales.

7. Customer Service: Excellent customer service is vital for your store's reputation. Be responsive to inquiries and offer hassle-free returns and refunds when needed.

8. Analytics and Optimization: Use analytics tools to track visitor behavior, sales, and other metrics. Analyze the data to make informed decisions and continuously optimize your store.

Success Story: The Rise of Shopify

Shopify is a prime example of the e-commerce boom. Founded in 2006, the company has grown into one of the leading e-commerce platforms, serving businesses of all sizes. With its user-friendly interface, customizable templates, and a range of features, Shopify empowers entrepreneurs to create their online stores quickly and efficiently.

Shopify provides a wide array of tools for inventory management, payment processing, and marketing, making it accessible to both newcomers and experienced e-commerce entrepreneurs. Moreover, the platform allows seamless integration with various payment gateways, enabling entrepreneurs to accept payments from customers around the world.

The company's success is not only attributed to its technology but also its community. Shopify has created a vast ecosystem of developers, designers, and marketers who contribute to the platform's growth. With over 1,700 apps available in the Shopify App Store, entrepreneurs can extend the functionality of their online stores.

The rise of Shopify showcases how e-commerce platforms can democratize online selling. It has enabled countless entrepreneurs to bring their ideas to life, reaching a global market and generating substantial revenue.

Dropshipping

Dropshipping is an e-commerce business model that eliminates the need to hold inventory. Instead, you partner with suppliers who directly ship products to your customers. It's a low-risk approach to e-commerce that appeals to those looking to start an online store without the burdens of warehousing and inventory management.

Exploring Dropshipping

1. Niche Selection: As with starting an online store, choosing the right niche is crucial. Research and identify products that have demand but are not overly competitive.

2. Supplier Selection: Find reliable dropshipping suppliers. Popular platforms like AliExpress, SaleHoo, and Oberlo can connect you with suppliers offering a range of products.

3. Online Store Setup: Set up your online store using an e-commerce platform like Shopify, which offers features tailored to dropshipping businesses.

4. Product Listings: Import products from your chosen suppliers to your store. Optimize product titles, descriptions, and images to make them appealing to potential customers.

5. Pricing Strategy: Determine your pricing strategy, considering factors like product cost, shipping fees, and your desired profit margin.

6. Marketing and Branding: Implement marketing strategies to attract customers to your store. Social media advertising, content marketing, and influencer collaborations can be effective.

7. Customer Service: Offer top-notch customer service, including addressing inquiries, handling returns, and ensuring timely product delivery.

8. Scaling Your Business: As your dropshipping business grows, consider expanding your product range, optimizing your marketing efforts, and potentially diversifying your suppliers.

Dropshipping is an attractive option for aspiring entrepreneurs because it requires minimal upfront investment. However, it's essential to understand that it can be a highly competitive space, and success often depends on your ability to find unique products, create an appealing brand, and effectively market your store.

Affiliate Marketing

Affiliate marketing is a performance-based marketing model in which individuals or affiliates earn a commission for promoting products or services of other companies. It's a versatile approach that can be incorporated into various online platforms and content.

Exploring Affiliate Marketing

1. **Affiliate Programs:** Join affiliate programs of companies and products you wish to promote. These programs provide you with unique affiliate links or tracking codes to identify your referrals.

2. **Content Creation:** Create content that incorporates affiliate links, such as blog posts, reviews, videos, or social media posts. Make sure your content is educational and delivers meaningful insights to your target audience.

3. **Target Audience:** Understand your target audience and choose affiliate products or services that align with their needs and interests.

4. **Promotion and Marketing:** Promote your content and affiliate links through various channels, including your website, social media, email newsletters, and paid advertising.

5. **Compliance and Disclosure:** Adhere to legal and ethical standards by clearly disclosing your affiliate relationships to your audience. Transparency builds trust.

6. **Analytics and Optimization:** Use tracking tools and analytics to measure the performance of your affiliate

marketing efforts. Optimize your strategies based on the data.

Success Story: The Power of Affiliate Marketing

Affiliate marketing has been instrumental in the success of numerous online entrepreneurs and bloggers. One example is Pat Flynn, the creator of Smart Passive Income, a blog and podcast that teaches others how to build successful online businesses.

Pat Flynn's journey into affiliate marketing began when he recommended products he personally used and believed in. He emphasized transparency and only endorsed products he found valuable. His genuine approach resonated with his audience, and he gradually built trust as an affiliate marketer.

One of Pat's significant achievements is his promotion of Bluehost, a web hosting service. Through his blog and podcast, he explained how Bluehost had helped him with his websites. His affiliate marketing efforts were successful, generating substantial commissions.

His success in affiliate marketing extended to other products and services. By consistently delivering high-quality content and building trust with his audience, Pat

Flynn's affiliate marketing income has become a significant source of revenue, earning him millions over the years.

The key takeaway from Pat's success is the importance of authenticity and trust in affiliate marketing. By genuinely believing in and advocating for products or services, affiliate marketers can build lasting relationships with their audience and achieve significant financial gains.

Print on Demand

Print on demand (POD) is a business model that allows you to create custom products, such as apparel, mugs, and posters, without the need for inventory or upfront costs. It's a popular choice for creatives and entrepreneurs looking to sell unique merchandise.

Exploring Print on Demand

1. **Design Creation:** Create or commission designs that can be printed on various products. These designs can be custom illustrations, graphics, quotes, or artwork.

2. **POD Platform Selection:** Choose a print on demand platform, such as Printful, Printify, or Teespring. These platforms manage every aspect, including the printing and shipping processes.

3. **Product Selection:** Decide which products you want to offer with your designs. Common options include T-shirts, hoodies, phone cases, posters, and home decor items.

4. **Online Store Integration:** Connect your chosen POD platform to your online store, which could be a Shopify store or a standalone e-commerce website.

5. **Customization:** Configure your product listings, allowing customers to select their preferred size, color, and design options.

6. **Marketing and Branding:** Market your products through social media, your website, and other online channels. Building a brand around your designs can set your store apart.

7. **Customer Engagement:** Engage with your customers by responding to inquiries and requests. Personalize the shopping experience.

8. **Quality Control:** Monitor the quality of the products to maintain high customer satisfaction. Some POD platforms offer sample orders to assess product quality.

Print on demand is an accessible way to turn your creativity into profit, and it eliminates the need for inventory management and order fulfillment. However, success in this space depends on your ability to create appealing designs, market your products effectively, and provide exceptional customer service.

Selling Digital Products

The digital age has given rise to a thriving market for digital products, such as e-books, courses, stock photos, and software. Selling digital products allows you to create once and sell repeatedly, making it a scalable online income option.

Exploring Selling Digital Products

1. **Product Creation:** Create or acquire digital products that cater to a specific audience's needs or interests. These products can include e-books, online courses, printables, stock media, templates, and software.

2. **E-commerce Platform:** Choose an e-commerce platform that supports the sale of digital products. Options include Gumroad, SendOwl, and WooCommerce with digital download extensions.

3. **Content Delivery:** Set up automated content delivery systems to ensure customers receive their digital products immediately after purchase.

4. **Pricing and Marketing:** Determine pricing for your digital products and develop a marketing strategy. Leverage content marketing, email marketing, and social media to reach your target audience.

5. **Customer Support:** Provide customer support for buyers who may have questions or encounter issues with their digital downloads.

6. **Update and Expand:** Regularly update and expand your digital product offerings to keep your business fresh and engaging for repeat customers.

Selling digital products can provide a consistent income stream, especially if you have expertise in a specific area or are capable of creating unique and valuable digital content. The key is to understand your audience's needs and tailor your products accordingly.

Chapter 4: The Mystique of Passive Wealth Streams

Passive income, the enigmatic realm of financial triumph, embodies the ethereal ideal of reaping riches without the ceaseless toil. In this chapter, we embark on a cryptic journey to unravel the diverse cryptograms that lead to passive prosperity, whether through the written word, the captivating screen, the mellifluous airwaves, the visual reveries, or the arcane alchemy of investing.

The Enigmatic World of Blogging and Content Alchemy

Blogging, once a humble parchment of personal thoughts, has metamorphosed into a transcendent cipher for information dissemination, community alchemy, and wealth conjuration. With the cryptic art of crafting consistently potent content and deciphering the secrets of monetization, bloggers can conjure consistent streams of passive prosperity.

Enigma of Blogging and Content Alchemy

1. **Niche Selection:** The cryptic choice of a niche must resonate with your arcane passions and expertise, yet

decode the enigmatic riddles of market demand and audience dimensions.

2. The Elixir of Quality Content: To beckon readers like enchanting sirens, consistently summon articles steeped in alchemical wisdom, scholarly allure, and engaging enchantment.

3. Monetary Transmutations:

  a. Ad Alchemy: Weave the spells of ad platforms like Google AdSense or Media.net into your blog's tapestry to conjure wealth through impressions and clicks.

  b. Affiliate Alchemy: Embrace the arcane dance of affiliate links to elicit commissions when readers, under your spell, procure goods or services.

  c. Sponsored Incantations: Forge allegiances with mysterious corporations and brands, conjuring sponsored posts and reviews like elusive enchantments.

  d. Digital Potions: Craft and distribute esoteric digital wares, be they enchanted e-books or bewitching online courses, to captivate your disciples.

e. **Membership and Subscription Alchemy:** Conceal premium content behind the sacred veil of subscription fees, thus granting your disciples exclusive access.

f. **Offerings and Crowdfunding:** Open the mystical gates for your patrons to offer alms through portals like Patreon or Ko-fi, like pilgrims on a sacred quest.

g. **The Arcane Sale of Tangibles**: Evoke physical products, like enchanted relics or mystical tomes, for your loyal fellowship to procure.

4. **SEO Mysticism and Enigmatic Promotion:** Invoke the ancient rites of SEO to beckon organic followers and employ the mystic forces of social media, email magic, and networking to unveil your blog's hidden essence.

5. **Engagement Alchemy:** Craft responses to the summons of your audience, fashioning a guild of devoted sycophants who will shield your arcane secrets.

6. **Analytics and the Alchemy of Optimization:** Study the scrolls of analytics to divine the performance of your blog, steering your ship with wisdom granted from the stars.

Tale of Enigma: The Mystical Scribe – Darren Rowse

Darren Rowse, a luminary in the arcane art of blogging, emerged as a pioneer from the mists of obscurity. His sanctified blog, ProBlogger, which materialized in the year 2004, has been a wellspring of wisdom for aspirants seeking to monetize their digital realms. Through the incantations of ceaseless and impeccable content, Darren Rowse fashioned a sanctified portal amidst the blogosphere's tempestuous seas.

Foremost among Rowse's enchantments is the alluring sorcery of affiliate marketing. He weaves his charms, endorsing products and services that resonate with his truth, revealing his affiliations to his acolytes. His tomes of digital wisdom, the esoteric ebooks and online courses, contribute to a river of uninterrupted prosperity.

Yet, another artifact of his journey lies in the creation of the ProBlogger convocation, a ceremonial gathering of blogging disciples and content creators. This spectral event emerged as both a treasure chest of riches and a nexus for occult networking, showcasing the myriad ways bloggers may beckon prosperity.

Rowse's chronicle signifies that birthing a blog and conjuring wealth from its cryptic depths entails diligence, patience, and an intimate familiarity with one's followers.

It is an odyssey rife with arcane rituals and evolving landscapes, a path only the most intrepid souls dare tread.

The Cryptic Secrets of YouTube and Video Alchemy

YouTube, the enigmatic realm where sound and image conjoin in beguiling sequences, emerges as both oracle and conduit for the sibylline art of wealth creation. In this enigmatic chapter, we shall explore the cryptic rituals of channel creation and the transmutation of videos into streams of passive affluence.

Exploring the Cryptic Realms of YouTube and Video Alchemy

1. **Choosing the Niche Nexus:** Aspiring sorcerers of the screen must select niches resonant with their passions, knowledge, and the yearnings of their targeted clans. The most potent channels often abide by a singular theme.

2. **The Enchantment of Content Craft:** Mages of video creation must summon high-quality content through enchanted lenses, crystal-clear microphones, and arcane editing scripts to amplify the spells they weave.

3. Monetary Transmutations:

a. YouTube Partner Pact: Initiate the YouTube Partner Program and conjure wealth through ad rites, dependent on viewings, clicks, and the passage of time.

b. Brand Covenants and Sponsorships: Forge alliances with corporate alchemists within your sphere for sponsorship incantations, where you shall be handsomely rewarded for the mystical promotion of their wares.

c. Merchandise Alchemy: Craft and purvey magical trinkets tied to your brand, be they enchanted garments or mystical talismans, through cryptic platforms such as Teespring or Printful.

d. Channel Membership Mysteries: Extend invitations to your ardent followers to join your mystical fellowship, offering arcane emotes, badges, and exclusive lore in exchange for monthly tributes.

e. Crowdfunding Conjurations: Encourage the viewers who walk your path to sow their silver through portals like Patreon or Ko-fi, supporting your mystical quest.

4. SEO Sorcery and Conjuration: Optimize the incantations of your video titles, descriptions, and tags to enhance your

discovery. Form alliances with fellow enchanters and take to social media for cross-promotion.

5. Engagement Alchemy: Respond to the messages of your followers, for it is through this communion that your bonds will be forged, and your power magnified.

6. The Elixir of Consistency: Regularity in your offerings is the key to growing your coven of followers. Stay true to the schedule you have inscribed in the scrolls of fate.

7. Analytical Divination and Optimization: Gaze into the mystical mirrors of YouTube's analytics tools, decode the omens, and adjust your practices accordingly.

Tale of Enigma: The Vagabond Enchanter - Casey Neistat

Casey Neistat, a vagabond enchanter of YouTube, wove daily spells of vlogs, film productions, and storytelling that mesmerized millions. His channel, a hallowed abode for millions of acolytes, exemplifies the potential of personal brands as sources of prodigious wealth.

Ad revenue, the most prominent spell in Neistat's grimoire, swelled as his channel grew in prominence. His brand sponsorships, forged with companies   in harmony with his magic, further replenished his enchanted coffers. Yet, he ventured beyond, conjuring his brand, 368, and crafting mystical relics that he sold to his devoted pilgrims.

The secret of Neistat's triumph resides in his authenticity and unwavering consistency. His heartfelt approach to content creation, his ability to engage his community, and the candor with which he communicated with his disciples set the stage for a thriving channel and a perennial wellspring of passive riches.

Podcasting – The Whispering Secrets of Passive Wealth

Podcasting, an auditory dimension where creators send their voices through the ether, has become a conduit to unravel the cryptic treasures of audience connection and wealth conjuration. This chapter unveils the enigmatic methods of starting a podcast and converting it into a river of passive affluence.

The Secrets of Podcasting Unveiled

1. Choosing the Whispers of Your Niche: Seek the enigmatic niches that resonate with your heart, wisdom, and the ears of your intended audience. The art of standing out in the podcast's whispered crowd is key.

2. Crafting Enchanting Soundscapes: Create sonorous and alluring episodes using mystical audio equipment and ethereal editing incantations to enhance your production value.

3. Monetary Transmutations:

  a. Sponsorship Incantations and Commercial Charms: Form mystic pacts with companies ensconced within your chosen realm for the bestowal of sponsorship wealth and advertising treasures.

  b. Affiliate Alchemy: Whisper in the ears of your listeners about products or services aligned with your essence, reaping commissions from the acquisitions made through your enchantments.

  c. Listener Patronage: Encourage your disciples to pledge their loyalty and resources through sacred platforms like Patreon, allowing them to bestow gifts regularly.

  d. Premium Enchantments: Offer premium or exclusive content to those who dare cross your monetary thresholds, revealing extra episodes or hidden treasures.

4. **SEO Whispers and Promotion Mysteries:** Etch runes of discovery on your podcast titles, descriptions, and episode tags. Foster your mystical presence on social media and form alliances with other conjurers in your chosen realm.

5. **Engagement Alchemy:** Interact with the whispers of your audience, for through these conversations, you shall craft a community of devotees to guard your secrets.

6. **The Elixir of Regularity:** Bestow a consistent schedule upon your enchantments, for it is this regularity that shall bind your disciples to you.

7. **Analytical Divinations and Optimization:** Gaze into the mystical mirrors of podcast analytics to decipher the omens, adjusting your future enunciations accordingly.

Tale of Enigma: The Whispering Chronicler – Serial Podcast

The podcast "Serial," a saga that unfurled in the year 2014, exemplifies the art of storytelling intertwined with journalism that captivated audiences and begot substantial riches through sponsorship and advertising. The clandestine chronicles unfolded in the world of true crime, beckoning an audience dedicated and engaged.

The treasure amassed by "Serial" was primarily through sponsorship and advertising. Companies, enchanted by the vast and captivated audience, sought to place their spells within the episodes, paying lavish tributes for their secret promotions.

"Serial" stands as an exemplar of weaving storytelling into journalism, capturing audiences in a narrative while unveiling true events. This enchanting sorcery drew both sponsors and listeners, demonstrating the potential of compelling content to generate substantial passive wealth.

The Enigma of Stock Photography and Video

The insatiable appetite for visual riches in marketing, advertising, and design has summoned opportunities for photographers and videographers to transform their visual creations into streams of passive affluence through the alchemy of stock platforms. This chapter unlocks the cryptic gateway to this domain.

Journeying into the Secrets of Stock Photography and Video

1. Capturing Visual Phantasms: Evoke exquisite photos and moving images through the lens of your mystical apparatus.

Invest in professional instruments and unlock the secrets of composition, light, and post-processing.

2. Keyword Alchemy and Metadata Spells: Decipher and inscribe enchanting keywords and metadata to your visual offerings, making them visible on stock platforms.

3. Platform Portals: Choose the stock photography and video portals to host your visual relics. The enchanted options include Shutterstock, Adobe Stock, Getty Images, and the enigmatic offspring of Shutterstock, iStock.

4. Offerings and Approval Conspiracies: Present your visual enhancements to the chosen portals, ensuring they meet the portals' quality and technical standards.

5. Licensing Enigmas: Familiarize yourself with the licensing incantations used by stock platforms, from the royalty-free to the rights-managed.

6. Promotion Elixirs: Amplify the allure of your portfolio through your personal portal, summoning winds of social media, and creating alliances to expand your reach.

7. Consistency Alchemy: Offer new visual treasures regularly, thus expanding your collection, for the more relics you have, the greater your potential for passive riches.

8. Watching and Optimizing Enchantments: Employ the divination tools bestowed by stock platforms to track the performance of your relics. Optimize your offerings guided by the omens.

Tale of Enigma: The Shutterstock Enchantment

Shutterstock, the sovereign of stock photography and video, conjured a global realm where photographers and videographers could barter their visual enchantments to businesses, artists, and individuals. Its chronicle stands as a testament to the immense potential of converting photographic or videographic magic into wealth.

Founded in 2003, Shutterstock burgeoned into a platform with millions of contributors and a colossal treasury of visual wealth. It has provided an avenue for photographers and videographers worldwide to earn tributes by licensing their relics.

One of the most intriguing aspects of Shutterstock's triumph lies in its adaptability to the shifting tides of the digital sea. The platform introduced innovative rites such as Shutterstock Select, an assembly of premium relics, catering to the evolving desires of seekers.

The potential income through Shutterstock is substantial for contributors who persistently supply high-quality relics. Success often hinges on interpreting market auguries and creating versatile and unique visual treasures.

Shutterstock's journey illuminates the unquenchable thirst for visual treasures and the opportunities available to those who seek passive wealth through their photographic and videographic conjurations.

Investing and Dividends: The Arcane Path to Passive Riches

Investing, a timeless and proven mechanism, presents the enigmatic path to passive riches. By allocating your resources with sagacity, you can erect an eclectic portfolio that generates returns through dividends, interest, and capital sorcery.

Voyaging through the Cryptic Realms of Investing and Dividends

1. **The Spellbook of Investment Knowledge:** Initiate your journey by absorbing the wisdom of diverse investment conduits. Comprehend the arcane arts of stocks, bonds, real estate, mutual funds, exchange-traded funds (ETFs), and other mysterious instruments.

2. **Riddles of Risk and Goals:** Appraise your appetite for risk and your ambitions in the art of investment. Decipher whether you seek a river of steady income, an empire of long-term growth, or a concoction of both.

3. **Diversification Sorcery:** Fragment your investments to distribute the risk. A diversified portfolio, adorned with stocks, bonds, and other enigmatic assets, may conjure balance.

4. **Stock Market Alchemy:** The art of investing in stocks, especially those bearing the gift of dividends, can furnish regular tributes to shareholders.

5. **Dividend Reinvestment Rituals (DRIPs):** Some corporations offer rituals known as Dividend Reinvestment Plans. Through these, you can command dividends to be reinvested in additional shares of the corporation's stock.

6. **The Alchemy of Real Estate:** Channel your wealth into real estate domains, whether they be abodes for lease or Real Estate Investment Trusts (REITs). Rental tributes and dividends from REITs offer paths to passive affluence.

7. **Bonds:** A Cryptic Script of Interest: Contemplate the mysteries of bonds, parchment bearing periodic interest for

those who hold it. Government bonds, municipal bonds, and corporate bonds offer domains to explore.

8. Mutual Funds and ETF Alchemy: Invest in the covenant of mutual funds or ETFs designed to conjure income. These mysteries typically contain a diverse trove of income-generating treasures.

9. A Timeless Perspective: Approach the art of investment with the wisdom of eternity. Passive riches often swell over the ages, as your holdings appreciate.

10. The Alchemist's Advisor: If the pathways of investment appear nebulous, consider summoning a financial sage to assist in crafting a script that aligns with your ambitions and risk tolerance.

Tale of Enigma: The Majesty of Dividend Investing

The saga of dividend investing unveils itself through the legends of companies known as "Dividend Aristocrats." These are entities that have consistently raised their dividend offerings for epochs. Among them stands Johnson & Johnson (J&J).

J&J, a multinational colossus in the realms of pharmaceuticals, consumer artifacts, and medical mystique, ascends to the grandeur of an S&P 500 Dividend Aristocrat. Its record of over half a century of ascending dividends beckons followers in search of passive riches.

Adherents who joined the J&J saga and held their script through the cycles have reaped the benefits of both dividend offerings and accrued wealth. The corporation's unbroken chain of dividend increments has enticed those who seek to amass assets as a source of regular passive tributes.

J&J's supremacy as a Dividend Aristocrat serves as a parable of the reliability and potentiality enshrined in dividend investing. By consecrating their wealth in companies that weave an unbroken chain of dividend growth, individuals can cultivate treasures that render a ceaseless source of passive affluence over time.

Chapter 5: The World of Online Work

In an increasingly connected world, online work and gig opportunities have emerged as versatile ways to earn money. This chapter explores various avenues for generating income through online services and gig work, including ride-sharing and delivery services, platforms like TaskRabbit, online surveys and market research, remote customer service, and social media management.

Ride-Sharing and Delivery Services

Ride-sharing and delivery services have transformed how people get around and receive goods. Platforms like Uber, Lyft, and DoorDash offer opportunities for individuals to earn money through driving and deliveries. Whether you have a car, a bicycle, or even just your feet, there's a gig opportunity for you.

Exploring Ride-Sharing and Delivery Services

1. Choosing a Platform: Select a ride-sharing or delivery platform available in your area and that suits your preferences. Popular options include Uber, Lyft, DoorDash, Uber Eats, Postmates, and Grubhub.

2. Vehicle and Equipment: Ensure you have the necessary vehicle or equipment. For ride-sharing, a car is essential, while some delivery platforms accept bicycles or scooters.

3. Registration and Checks: Sign up as a driver or delivery person with your chosen platform. Be prepared for background checks, vehicle inspections, and meeting specific requirements.

4. Setting Availability: Determine your working hours and availability. Many platforms offer flexible scheduling, allowing you to work when it's convenient for you.

5. Using the App: Familiarize yourself with the platform's app for navigation, managing orders, and communicating with customers.

6. Safety and Service: Prioritize safety while driving or making deliveries. Maintain good customer service to earn positive reviews and tips.

7. Earnings and Payments: Understand how the platform pays you. You can earn from ride fares, delivery fees, and customer tips, with payouts usually on a weekly or instant basis.

8. **Tax Considerations:** Keep records of your earnings and expenses for tax purposes. Many gig workers are classified as independent contractors and are responsible for their own taxes.

Success Story: Uber's Ride-Sharing Revolution

Uber, founded in 2009, has revolutionized the global ride-sharing market. It disrupted traditional taxi services by connecting riders with drivers through a user-friendly app. Uber's success demonstrates the potential of ride-sharing as a gig work opportunity.

Uber's advanced app allows riders to request rides and drivers to accept and navigate to those requests, creating a seamless experience for both parties and contributing to the platform's rapid growth.

Uber has provided countless individuals with the opportunity to earn income as drivers. It offers flexibility, allowing drivers to work according to their schedules, turning spare time or underutilized vehicles into a source of income.

Uber's influence extended to other services, such as Uber Eats for food delivery and Uber Freight for shipping and logistics. Diversifying its services created even more gig work opportunities and income potential.

Uber's story highlights how technology can reshape traditional industries, opening new doors for gig work and income opportunities. Success in ride-sharing and delivery services relies on safety, good customer service, and efficient use of the platform's tools.

TaskRabbit and Gig Economy Platforms

TaskRabbit is one of many gig economy platforms that connect people who need tasks done with individuals who can complete them. These tasks can range from assembling furniture to doing household chores, providing a wide variety of gig work opportunities.

Exploring TaskRabbit and Gig Economy Platforms

1. **Registration and Profile:** Sign up on platforms like TaskRabbit and create a profile showcasing your skills, experience, and availability.

2. **Task Selection:** Browse task listings posted by people needing help and choose those that match your skills and interests.

3. **Agreement and Communication:** Communicate with the task poster to understand requirements and agree on task details, including rates.

4. **Task Completion:** Fulfill the task as agreed, focusing on quality work to earn good reviews and recommendations.

5. **Payments and Fees:** TaskRabbit and similar platforms manage payments, often with a service fee or commission deducted before payout.

6. **Safety and Ratings:** Maintain a strong focus on safety and professionalism. High ratings and positive reviews can lead to more task opportunities.

7. **Tax Obligations:** Keep records of your earnings for tax purposes. Some gig workers are considered independent contractors, making them responsible for their own taxes.

8. Expanding Services: Consider offering a range of services on gig economy platforms to increase your income opportunities, such as moving assistance or event planning.

Success Story: TaskRabbit – The Pioneer of Task-Based Gig Work

TaskRabbit, founded in 2008, is a pioneer in the gig economy. It connects individuals with specific tasks or jobs that need to be completed. TaskRabbit's success reflects the demand for flexible gig work opportunities.

TaskRabbit's growth is attributed to its platform's versatility, making it convenient for both task posters and taskers. It allows individuals to outsource tasks they lack the skills or time to complete.

One key to TaskRabbit's success is its emphasis on safety and security, with identity verification, background checks, and insurance coverage for tasks, fostering trust between users.

TaskRabbit's influence extends to similar gig economy platforms, highlighting the potential for individuals to earn income by offering their skills and services in a flexible manner. It exemplifies the evolving nature of work, where individuals can take on diverse tasks based on their abilities and availability.

Online Surveys and Market Research

Online surveys and market research offer a unique way to earn money by providing your opinions and insights. Companies pay for consumer feedback and data, making it a straightforward gig work option.

Exploring Online Surveys and Market Research

1. Platform Selection: Sign up for online survey and market research platforms. Popular options include Survey Junkie, Swagbucks, and Vindale Research.

2. Profile Setup: Complete your profile with accurate demographic information to match you with relevant surveys and research opportunities.

3. Participation: Engage in surveys and market research studies as they become available. Some platforms offer daily opportunities.

4. **Earnings and Payouts:** Earn points or cash rewards for completing surveys and participating in research, often with a minimum payout threshold.

5. **Referral Programs:** Many platforms offer referral programs. Encourage friends and family to join for additional rewards on successful referrals.

6. **Time Management:** Dedicate time to complete surveys and research. Manage your schedule effectively to balance this gig work.

7. **Data Privacy:** Protect your data. Share information only with reputable platforms and avoid any suspicious survey or research opportunities.

8. **Multiple Platforms**: Sign up for multiple survey and research platforms to maximize your income potential.

Success Story: Swagbucks – Earning Rewards for Everyday Activities

Swagbucks allows users to earn rewards for various online activities, including surveys, watching videos, shopping online, and web searches. It demonstrates how individuals can accumulate income and rewards by integrating these activities into their daily routine.

Swagbucks users are encouraged to explore various earning options, from surveys and offers to watching videos and playing games. The platform's referral program provides additional income potential by inviting friends and family to join.

Swagbucks' story emphasizes the value of time and engagement in the gig economy. By dedicating time to complete tasks and earn rewards through online activities, users can accumulate income. The key is consistency and integrating these tasks into one's daily routine.

Remote Customer Service

Remote customer service has gained popularity in the digital age. Platforms like LiveOps and Arise offer opportunities for individuals to work as remote customer service agents, assisting customers from their own homes.

Exploring Remote Customer Service

1. **Platform Selection:** Choose a remote customer service platform that suits your skills and availability, such as LiveOps, Arise, or Amazon's Virtual Customer Service.

2. **Application and Onboarding**: Apply to become a remote customer service agent and undergo onboarding, which may include training and background checks.

3. **Equipment and Workspace**: Ensure you have essential equipment, like a computer and headset, and a quiet workspace for clear communication with customers.

4. **Availability and Scheduling**: Set your work hours, often with flexible scheduling on remote customer service platforms.

5. **Customer Support**: Provide excellent support by addressing inquiries, resolving issues, and maintaining professionalism.

6. **Earnings and Payments**: Understand the payment structure, which typically includes hourly or per-minute rates for talk time.

7. **Performance Metrics**: Monitor performance metrics like response time and customer satisfaction to open up more opportunities.

8. **Professional Development**: Consider ongoing training to improve your customer service skills and qualifications.

LiveOps, founded in 2001, is a pioneer in remote customer service. It provides businesses with a flexible remote customer service workforce, allowing companies to meet customer support needs without physical call centers.

LiveOps' gig work model benefits both businesses and remote agents, offering businesses an on-demand workforce and remote agents flexibility to work from home and set their schedules.

LiveOps' story illustrates the potential of remote customer service as a gig work opportunity, paving the way for other platforms and companies to explore the advantages of a remote, on-demand customer service workforce.

Social Media Management

Social media management has become crucial for businesses to enhance their brand presence. This has led to gig work opportunities for individuals to manage social media accounts and content creation.

1. **Skill Development:** Hone your social media management skills by learning about different platforms, content creation, and analytics.

2. **Client Acquisition:** Find clients who need social media management services, such as small businesses or startups.

3. **Content Creation:** Create engaging social media content tailored to each client's specific audience and goals.

4. **Scheduling and Analytics:** Use social media management tools to schedule posts, analyze engagement, and monitor campaign performance.

5. **Client Communication:** Maintain clear communication with clients to understand their expectations and goals.

6. **Payment Structure:** Determine your payment structure, whether hourly, monthly, or project-based, aligning it with the value you provide.

7. **Growth and Expansion:** As you gain experience, expand your client base and services for increased income opportunities.

The demand for effective social media management has led to the rise of social media management agencies. Hootsuite, for instance, offers comprehensive social media services for businesses and organizations. It allows users to schedule and publish posts, engage with their audience, and access analytics, streamlining social media efforts.

Social media management agencies highlight the significance of social media in modern business and marketing. Effective social media management can lead to increased brand visibility, engagement, and revenue growth.

Chapter 6: Real Estate and Investments

Investing in real estate and financial markets is a proven way to build wealth and earn money without working actively. In this chapter, we'll look at different methods for making money, like real estate crowdfunding, stock trading, day trading, peer-to-peer lending, and investing in cryptocurrencies and blockchain.

Real Estate Crowdfunding

Traditional real estate investments often require a lot of money and time. Real estate crowdfunding has made it easier for everyday people to invest in properties with less money and without the need for hands-on management.

Real Estate Crowdfunding Basics

1. **Choose a Platform:** Pick a real estate crowdfunding platform that suits your investment goals and risk tolerance. Platforms like Fundrise, RealtyMogul, and Crowdstreet are popular options.

2. **Create an Account:** Sign up on the platform, complete your profile, and provide the necessary information.

3. **Explore Investments**: Browse through the available investment opportunities. You'll find information about the property, location, expected returns, and the minimum investment amount.

4. **Choose Investments**: Select an investment that matches your goals and budget. Some platforms allow you to invest in multiple properties for diversification.

5. **Review Documents**: Carefully read the legal documents related to your chosen investment.

6. **Fund the Investment**: Invest your money through the platform. The platform will handle the property management and distribute returns.

7. **Monitor and Earn**: Keep an eye on your investments and get regular updates. These investments can yield passive income.

8. **Diversify**: As you gain experience and resources, consider spreading your investments across various properties and locations.

Success Story: Fundrise – Making Real Estate Accessible

Fundrise is a leading player in real estate crowdfunding, providing a way for individuals to invest in a mix of real estate assets. Their success shows how everyday people can build wealth and earn passive income.

Fundrise's strong point is diversification. They offer various investment options, including eREITs (electronic real estate investment trusts) and eFunds (electronic real estate funds), allowing investors to spread their capital across different properties and markets, which helps reduce risk.

Low fees and transparent communication have also contributed to Fundrise's success. They keep costs low, which means more profits for investors. They also provide regular updates, so investors always know how their investments are performing.

Fundrise's story highlights the potential of real estate crowdfunding and the advantages of diversification and clear communication for success in passive income generation.

Stock Trading and Day Trading

Stock trading, buying and selling shares of publicly traded companies, is a classic way to invest and potentially make money. Day trading is a more active and short-term approach to stock trading.

Stock Trading and Day Trading Basics

Stock Trading:

1. **Learn About Stocks**: Start by understanding how stock markets work and different investment strategies. Books, online courses, and financial news are great resources.

2. **Choose a Broker**: Pick a reputable online stock brokerage like E*TRADE, Charles Schwab, or TD Ameritrade.

3. **Set Up an Account**: Open a brokerage account and deposit funds for trading.

4. **Select Stocks**: Analyze and choose stocks that align with your strategy, considering company fundamentals and trends.

5. **Place Orders**: Use your brokerage platform to place buy and sell orders based on your strategy.

6. **Manage Risk**: Implement risk management strategies, such as setting stop-loss orders.

7. **Monitor and Analyze:** Keep an eye on your investments and stay informed about market news.

8. **Long-Term Perspective:** Think about holding stocks for the long term to benefit from potential capital appreciation and dividends.

Day Trading:

1. **Get Educated:** Day trading requires specific skills. Learn and consider practicing without real money first.

2. **Choose a Platform:** Select a day trading platform with real-time data. Thinkorswim and TradeStation are examples.

3. **Set Up an Account:** Open a day trading account with a brokerage that serves active traders.

4. **Manage Risk:** Follow strict risk management rules and stick to your strategy.

5. **Develop a Strategy:** Create a day trading strategy based on your risk tolerance and capital.

6. Use Technical Analysis: Master chart analysis and technical indicators to spot potential entry and exit points.

7. Execute Trades: Execute trades quickly according to your strategy.

8. Stay Calm: Keep your emotions in check, as day trading can be stressful. Stick to your strategy.
Success Story: Warren Buffett – The Investment Legend

Warren Buffett is often considered one of the most successful investors globally, showcasing the potential of stock trading and long-term wealth accumulation.

Buffett's success comes from his value investing approach. He buys shares of companies with strong fundamentals and holds them for extended periods, leading to capital appreciation and dividend income. His investment in Berkshire Hathaway, a conglomerate with interests in various industries, demonstrates the benefits of identifying undervalued companies and managing a diversified portfolio.

Buffett's story emphasizes the passive income potential of stock trading, especially when taking a long-term perspective and focusing on companies with solid fundamentals. As you explore stock trading, think about patient and informed decision-making.

Peer-to-Peer Lending

Peer-to-peer (P2P) lending is an alternative way to make money by lending your money to borrowers through online platforms and earning interest on your loans.

Peer-to-Peer Lending Basics

1. **Select a Platform:** Choose a P2P lending platform matching your risk tolerance and lending criteria, like LendingClub or Prosper.

2. **Create an Account:** Sign up on the chosen platform, complete your profile, and provide necessary information.

3. **Choose Loans:** Browse available loans and select the ones you want to fund. Loans come with borrower profiles, purposes, and interest rates.

4. **Investment Amount:** Decide how much to lend to each borrower, diversifying your investments for lower risk.

5. **Evaluate Risk:** Assess borrower risk by checking their credit profile and platform-provided information.

6. Fund Loans: Provide funds for the chosen loans, and the platform manages loan servicing.

7. Get Returns: Earn interest on your loans as borrowers make repayments. Reinvesting can help maximize your income.

8. Diversify More: Broaden your P2P lending portfolio by lending to various borrowers and loan types.

Success Story: LendingClub – The P2P Lending Pioneer

LendingClub is a pioneer in the P2P lending industry, showing how individuals can earn money by lending to others. Founded in 2006, it matches lenders with borrowers seamlessly.

LendingClub's success lies in diversification. It offers various investment options, and investors can diversify by investing in fractions of different loans across different borrowers, which spreads the risk.

LendingClub also keeps fees low and provides regular updates, keeping investors informed about their investments' performance.

LendingClub's story emphasizes the income potential of P2P lending, highlighting the importance of risk management and diversification in earning money.

Cryptocurrency and Blockchain Investments

Cryptocurrency and blockchain technology have shaken up traditional finance. They offer new investment opportunities, but they also come with risks.

Cryptocurrency and Blockchain Investment Basics

1. **Learn About Cryptos:** Begin by understanding cryptocurrencies and blockchain technology. Knowing the basics is essential.

2. **Get a Wallet:** Secure a cryptocurrency wallet to store your digital assets safely.

3. **Choose an Exchange:** Sign up on a reputable cryptocurrency exchange like Coinbase or Binance.

4.   Diversify: Consider investing in various cryptocurrencies, from established ones like Bitcoin to promising altcoins.

5. Manage Risk: Cryptocurrency markets can be volatile. Use strategies like stop-loss orders and only invest what you can afford to lose.

6. Long-Term Hold: For some cryptos, a long-term holding strategy may be the way to go.

7. Staking and Yield Farming: Explore opportunities for passive income through staking or yield farming.

8. Prioritize Security: Keep your crypto secure with strong passwords and two-factor authentication.

9. Stay Informed: Keep up with crypto news, market analysis, and technology developments. Do your research before investing in new projects.

Success Story: The Rise of Bitcoin

Bitcoin, the pioneer of cryptocurrencies, is a symbol of the crypto revolution. Its journey from obscurity to a global digital asset shows the potential for wealth accumulation and passive income.

Bitcoin's success comes from its groundbreaking technology and decentralized nature. Operating on a blockchain, it's a secure digital ledger. Its limited supply has made it valuable over time.

Investors who recognized Bitcoin's potential early experienced significant returns. As you delve into cryptocurrencies, keep in mind the risks associated with their high volatility.

Chapter 7: Success Strategies

Online income generation, whether through freelancing or investments, is more than just knowing the basics. Success depends on how you approach it, your mindset, and your strategies. In this chapter, we'll delve into key tips and principles to excel in your online income endeavors.

Realistic Goals

Achieving success in any income-generating venture starts with setting clear, achievable goals. Whether you're freelancing, running an online store, or investing, having a roadmap keeps you motivated and on track.

SMART Goals

- Specific: Define your goals clearly. Instead of saying, "I want to make money from my blog," say, "I want to earn $500 per month from my blog through affiliate marketing within the next six months."

- Measurable: Make your goals quantifiable, allowing you to track progress. For example, "earn $500 per month" is measurable.

- **Achievable**: Ensure your goals are realistic. Earning $10,000 per month from a new blog in a month might not be realistic, but working up to it over a year could be.

- **Relevant:** Align your goals with your overall objectives. If freelancing is your focus, setting a blogging goal may not be relevant.

- **Time-Bound:** Set deadlines for your goals. This creates urgency and helps you prioritize tasks. For instance, "within the next six months" sets a clear timeframe.

Breaking Down Long-Term Goals

Long-term goals can seem daunting, but breaking them into smaller, manageable steps makes them less overwhelming. If your long-term goal is to earn $100,000 per year from your e-commerce store, break it down into monthly or quarterly milestones.

Tracking Progress

Regularly monitor your progress toward your goals. This helps you stay focused and adjust your strategy if needed. If you're falling short of a monthly income target, analyze what's not working and make changes.

Time Management and Productivity

Effective time management and productivity are essential for online income generation. Many online income paths require self-discipline and making the most of your time.

Time Management Strategies

- **Prioritize Tasks:** Identify and tackle the most important and urgent tasks first.

- **Set a Schedule:** Establish a daily or weekly schedule to allocate time for work, personal life, and relaxation.

- **Time Blocks:** Allocate specific time blocks for particular tasks to maintain focus.

- **Avoid Multitasking:** Focus on one task at a time. Multitasking often reduces efficiency and work quality.

- **Use Tools and Apps:** Numerous time management apps and tools can help you plan and track your work.

- **Learn to Say No:** Avoid overcommitting and taking on too much work. Saying no can protect your schedule.

Productivity Techniques

- **Pomodoro Technique:** Work for a set time (usually 25 minutes), followed by a short break. It boosts productivity and focus.

- **Eisenhower Matrix:** Prioritize tasks by urgency and importance, sorting them into four categories: Do First, Schedule, Delegate, and Don't Do.

- **GTD (Getting Things Done):** Capture all your tasks and organize them into lists, contexts, and projects for better control and execution.

- **Batching**: Group similar tasks and handle them in one go. For example, answer all your emails in a designated email block.

- **Task Lists**: Maintain a daily or weekly task list to keep track of your work. To-do apps or paper lists are effective tools.

Marketing and Promotion

For many online income avenues, marketing and promotion are crucial for attracting customers, clients, or an audience. Effective marketing can significantly impact your success.

Key Marketing Principles

- **Know Your Audience:** Understand your target audience's needs, preferences, and pain points. Tailor your marketing efforts to address these factors.

- **Consistency:** Consistency in branding and messaging builds trust. Maintain a cohesive online presence.

- **Content Marketing:** Create valuable content that educates, entertains, or solves problems for your audience. Quality content attracts and retains visitors.

- **Search Engine Optimization (SEO):** Learn the basics of SEO to improve your website's visibility in search engines.

- **Social Media Engagement:** Use social media platforms to engage with your audience, share content, and build a community around your brand.

- **Email Marketing**: Build and maintain an email list to connect directly with your audience, a powerful tool for driving sales and engagement.

- **Networking**: Network with others in your industry. Building relationships can lead to collaboration and business opportunities.

Managing Finances and Taxes

Properly managing finances and understanding tax obligations are critical for long-term success in online income generation. Neglecting financial aspects can lead to challenges and legal issues.

Financial Management Tips

- **Budgeting:** Create a budget to track your income and expenses, helping you make informed financial decisions.

- **Separate Business and Personal Finances**: Maintain separate accounts for personal and business finances.

- **Emergency Fund:** Have an emergency fund to cover unexpected expenses, ensuring financial stability.

- **Savings and Investment:** Allocate a portion of your income for savings and investments to grow your wealth over time.

- **Debt Management:** Be mindful of your debts, especially high-interest ones, and work on reducing them.

- **Professional Advice:** For complex financial situations, consult a financial advisor or accountant for guidance.

Tax Considerations

- **Income Reporting:** Accurately report all income, including freelance income, online sales, and investment gains.

- **Deductions:** Learn about tax deductions and credits applicable to your income sources.

- **Quarterly Payments:** If you're self-employed, you may need to make quarterly estimated tax payments.

- **Keep Records:** Maintain detailed records of income, expenses, and receipts, essential for tax purposes.

- **Consult a Tax Professional**: Tax laws can be complex; a tax professional can help you navigate your tax obligations efficiently.

Staying Motivated and Persistent

Online income generation can be rewarding, but it also presents challenges. Staying motivated and persistent is vital for long-term success.

Tips for Staying Motivated

- **Set Milestones**: Celebrate small achievements along the way to your goals. Recognizing progress can be motivating.

- **Visualize Success**: Create a vision board or regularly visualize your successful future. This can boost motivation.

- **Find a Support System**: Connect with peers or mentors who can offer support and encouragement.

- **Take Breaks**: Avoid burnout by taking regular breaks to recharge and relax.

- **Stay Informed**: Keep learning and stay updated in your field. Knowledge and growth can be motivating.

- **Adaptability**: Be open to change and adapt to new trends and opportunities. Flexibility can keep you competitive.

- **Resilience**: Expect setbacks and failures, and develop resilience to bounce back and keep moving forward.

- **Routine**: Establish a work routine with regular tasks and goals to maintain a sense of purpose and direction.

- **Mindset**: Cultivate a growth mindset. Embrace challenges and view failures as learning opportunities.

- **Long-Term Perspective**: Remember that success often takes time. Be patient and committed to the journey.

Success Story: The Resilience of Walt Disney

Walt Disney, the founder of Disney, is a shining example of how persistence and resilience can lead to extraordinary success. Disney faced numerous setbacks and rejections in his early career, including being fired from a newspaper for a perceived lack of imagination. However, he persisted and created one of the most iconic entertainment empires in the world.

Disney's resilience and unwavering belief in his creative vision were pivotal in his success. His ability to adapt to new technologies, like sound in animation with "Steamboat Willie," further contributed to his achievements.

Disney's story serves as a reminder that even the most successful individuals face obstacles and rejections. What sets them apart is their determination to overcome adversity and continue pursuing their goals. As you work toward your online income goals, take inspiration from Disney's journey and approach challenges with resilience and persistence.

NOTE:
Success in online income generation isn't just about your chosen method; it's about your approach. Setting realistic goals, managing time effectively, mastering marketing, handling finances and taxes, and maintaining motivation and persistence are all vital for a successful online income journey.

By applying the principles and tips explored in this chapter, you can enhance your chances of success in your chosen online income avenue. Remember that success often requires adaptability, continuous learning, and the ability to navigate challenges and setbacks. Stay focused, stay motivated, and persist in your pursuit of online income. Your efforts can lead to a fulfilling and financially rewarding journey in the digital world.

Chapter 8: Key Steps for Success

Achieving success in online income generation requires various elements to fall into place. This chapter uncovers pivotal tips that can have a significant impact on your journey to success in diverse online income opportunities. From setting crystal clear objectives and effectively managing your time to marketing your offerings, handling finances, and preserving your motivation and perseverance, these principles are essential for those aiming to excel in the digital domain.

Setting Attainable Goals

Laying down clear and achievable goals is the bedrock of success in any income-generating pursuit. It offers direction, motivation, and a purpose-driven approach. When establishing your goals, consider adhering to the SMART framework:

- Specific: Define your goals in detail. Instead of saying, "I want to make money from my blog," say, "I aim to earn $500 per month from my blog through affiliate marketing in the next six months."

-**Measurable:** Your goals should be quantifiable, enabling you to monitor your progress. For instance, "earn $500 per month" is a measurable target.

- **Achievable:** Make sure your goals are realistic and within reach. While earning $10,000 per month from a brand-new blog in one month may be out of reach, reaching that level over a year could be feasible.

- **Relevant:** Ensure that your goals align with your overall objectives. If your primary focus is freelancing, setting a goal related to blogging may not be pertinent.

- **Time-Bound:** Set deadlines for your goals to create urgency and prioritize tasks. "Within the next six months" provides a clear timeframe in the example above.

Breaking Down Long-Term Goals

Long-term goals can often seem overwhelming. To make them more digestible, break them into smaller, actionable steps. For example, if your long-term goal is to earn $100,000 annually from your e-commerce store, you can set monthly or quarterly milestones.

Tracking Progress

Frequently monitor your progress toward your goals. This practice helps you remain focused and adapt your strategy if you're falling short of monthly income targets. Analyze what's not working and make the necessary changes.

Time Management and Efficiency

Effective time management and efficiency are paramount for online income generation. Many online income avenues necessitate self-discipline and making the most of the available time.

Time Management Strategies

-**Prioritize Tasks**: Identify and tackle the most important and urgent tasks first. The Eisenhower Matrix can be a valuable tool for effective prioritization.

- **Set a Schedule:** Develop a daily or weekly schedule that allocates time for work, personal life, and relaxation. Adhering to a schedule can heighten your productivity.

- **Use Time Blocks:** Time blocking involves allocating specific blocks of time to particular tasks. This method aids in maintaining focus and eliminating distractions.

- **Avoid Multitasking**: Concentrate on one task at a time. Multitasking often diminishes efficiency and the quality of work.

- **Use Tools and Apps**: Numerous time management apps and tools can help you plan, track, and optimize your work.

- **Learn to Say No**: Evade overcommitting and taking on excessive tasks. Saying no to additional work can safeguard your schedule.

Efficiency Techniques

- **Pomodoro Technique**: This time management approach involves working for a set time (typically 25 minutes), followed by a brief break. It can boost productivity and help you remain focused.

- **GTD (Getting Things Done)**: The GTD method revolves around capturing all your to-dos and organizing them into lists, contexts, and projects for better control and execution.

- **Eisenhower Matrix**: Prioritize tasks based on urgency and importance, sorting them into categories like Do First, Schedule, Delegate, and Don't Do.

- **Batching**: Group similar tasks and handle them all at once. For example, allocate a specific time block to respond to emails rather than addressing them sporadically throughout the day.

- **Task Lists**: Keep a daily or weekly task list to monitor your work. Whether you use to-do apps or simple paper lists, this can be an effective practice.

Marketing and Promotion

In many online income avenues, marketing and promotion are indispensable. Effective marketing can substantially influence your success by drawing customers, clients, or an audience.

Key Marketing Principles

- **Know Your Audience**: Grasping your target audience's needs, preferences, and pain points is critical. Tailor your marketing efforts to effectively address these factors.

- **Consistency**: Upholding consistency in your branding and messaging fosters trust. Sustaining a unified and dependable online presence is imperative.

- **Content Marketing**: Generating valuable content that educates, entertains, or solves problems for your audience is key. Quality content attracts and retains visitors.

- **Search Engine Optimization (SEO)**: Gaining proficiency in the fundamentals of SEO can enhance your website's visibility in search engines, thereby increasing your chances of organic traffic.

- **Social Media Engagement:** Leveraging social media platforms to interact with your audience, share content, and build a community around your brand is pivotal.

- **Email Marketing:** Building and maintaining an email list allows direct communication with your audience, a potent tool for driving sales and engagement.

- **Networking:** Establishing connections with others in your industry can lead to collaborations and business opportunities. Building relationships is fundamental.

Managing Finances and Taxes

Prudent financial management and comprehending your tax responsibilities are indispensable for long-term success in online income generation. Neglecting financial aspects can lead to challenges and legal complications.

Financial Management Tips

- **Budgeting:** Create a budget to monitor your income and expenses. This practice helps you make informed financial decisions and ensures your financial stability.

- **Separate Business and Personal Finances:** If you run a business or generate income online, it's critical to maintain separate accounts for personal and business finances.

- **Emergency Fund:** Maintaining an emergency fund to cover unexpected expenses is a prudent choice. Financial stability is vital for your peace of mind.

- **Savings and Investment:** Allocate a portion of your income for savings and investments. This strategy can help you grow your wealth over time and secure your financial future.

- **Debt Management:** Be mindful of your debts and work on reducing them, especially high-interest debts. Reducing debt can free up more of your income for other uses.

- **Professional Advice:** In cases where your financial situation becomes complex, consider consulting a financial advisor or accountant for guidance. They can offer valuable insights for informed decision-making.

Tax Considerations

- **Income Reporting:** Ensure you accurately report all income, including freelance income, online sales, and investment gains. Accurate reporting is essential to remain compliant with tax laws.

- **Deductions:** Familiarize yourself with tax deductions and credits that apply to your income sources. Utilizing these deductions can lower your overall tax liability.

- **Quarterly Payments:** If you're self-employed, you may need to make quarterly estimated tax payments to cover your annual tax liability. Paying these estimates ensures you avoid penalties and surprises when it's time to file your taxes.

- **Keep Records:** Maintain detailed records of income, expenses, and receipts. These records are vital for tax purposes and can substantiate your deductions and credits.

- **Consult a Tax Professional:** Tax laws can be intricate and subject to changes. If you're uncertain about your tax obligations or the most advantageous strategies for your specific situation, consider consulting a tax professional.

Staying Motivated and Persevering

Online income generation can be a rewarding yet challenging journey. Maintaining motivation and perseverance is crucial for long-term success.

Tips for Staying Motivated

- **Set Milestones:** Celebrate minor achievements along your journey. Recognizing progress can boost motivation and instill a sense of accomplishment.

- **Visualize Success:** Create a vision board or regularly envision your prosperous future. Visualization can heighten motivation and keep you focused on your goals.

- **Find a Support System:** Connect with peers or mentors who can provide support and encouragement. Sharing your challenges and successes with others can be motivating.

- **Take Breaks:** Avoid burnout by taking regular breaks to recharge and relax. Burnout can deplete your motivation and creativity, so self-care is vital.

- **Stay Informed:** Keep learning and stay updated in your field. Knowledge and growth can be motivating as they open new doors and opportunities.

Tips for Perseverance

- **Adaptability:** Be open to change and adapt to new trends and opportunities. Flexibility can keep you competitive and relevant in your chosen field.

- **Resilience:** Anticipate setbacks and failures, and cultivate resilience to bounce back and keep progressing. Resilience is often the key to overcoming challenges.

- **Routine:** Establish a work routine that includes regular tasks and goals to maintain a sense of purpose and direction. Routines can help maintain consistency and productivity.

- **Mindset:** Cultivate a growth mindset. Embrace challenges and view failures as opportunities to learn and improve. A positive mindset can make a significant difference.

- **Long-Term Perspective**: Success often takes time. Be patient and committed to the journey, even when facing obstacles. A long-term perspective can keep you on track.

Success Story: The Resilience of Walt Disney

Walt Disney, the founder of Disney, exemplifies how persistence and resilience can lead to extraordinary success. Disney faced numerous setbacks and rejections in his early career. He was once fired from a newspaper for lacking imagination and creativity. However, he persisted and went on to create one of the most iconic entertainment empires globally.

Disney's resilience and unwavering belief in his creative vision were pivotal in his success. His ability to adapt to new technologies, such as the introduction of sound in animation (Steamboat Willie was a groundbreaking cartoon), further contributed to his achievements.

Disney's story serves as a reminder that even the most successful individuals face obstacles and rejections. What sets them apart is their determination to overcome adversity and continue pursuing their goals. As you work toward your online income goals, take inspiration from Disney's journey and approach challenges with resilience and persistence.

Success in online income generation isn't solely about the specific method you choose but also about how you approach your endeavors. By applying the principles and tips explored in this chapter, you can enhance your chances of success in your chosen online income avenue.

Whether you're freelancing, selling products or services online, investing, or pursuing any other form of online income, remember that success often requires adaptability, continuous learning, and the ability to navigate challenges and setbacks. Stay focused, stay motivated, and persist in your pursuit of online income. Your efforts can lead to a fulfilling and financially rewarding journey in the digital world.

Your journey toward online income generation is a unique and evolving one. However, the principles outlined in this chapter can provide you with a solid foundation and guide you on your path to success. Stay motivated, persistent, and adaptable, and continue to learn and grow in your chosen field. Your determination and effort can lead to remarkable achievements in the digital world.

Chapter 9: The Conclusion

As we wrap up our exploration of online income generation, it's important to take a moment to reflect on what we've learned in this guide. The digital world provides numerous opportunities to make money, whether you're freelancing, running an online store, investing, or exploring other ways to generate income. This chapter serves as a summary and offers some final thoughts to guide you on your journey to success in the world of online income.

The Diverse World of Online Income

One significant lesson we've learned is that online income generation comes in many forms. There are countless ways to make money online, each with its own set of opportunities and challenges. Whether you choose freelancing, e-commerce, investing, or any other method, the possibilities are vast.

What truly matters is finding an approach that matches your skills, interests, and financial goals. Online income should be a journey that you find satisfying and meaningful.

The Power of Technology and the Internet

The internet and modern technology have revolutionized how we work and earn a living. Thanks to the global reach of the internet, you can connect with clients, customers, and investors from all over the world. Online platforms and tools have made it easier than ever to start a business, showcase your skills, or invest in various assets.

Embracing these technological advances is crucial for success in the digital age. Whether you're building a website for your online store, creating content for a blog, or managing your investment portfolio through an app, technology is your ally.

The Importance of Adaptability and Learning

In the fast-paced digital world, being adaptable and continuously learning is essential. Trends and technologies evolve rapidly, and what works today might not be effective tomorrow. This emphasizes the need to stay informed, acquire new skills, and be open to change.

It's crucial to keep an eye on market trends, emerging technologies, and shifts in consumer behavior. Your ability to adapt and stay ahead can set you apart from the competition and ensure long-term success.

The Role of Patience and Persistence

Success in online income generation often requires patience and persistence. Obstacles and setbacks are common, whether you're building a brand, growing a blog, or investing in stocks. It's during these moments that patience and persistence become your greatest assets.

Take inspiration from the stories of successful individuals who faced adversity but never gave up. Remember that the path to success is seldom straightforward, and setbacks are opportunities for growth and learning.

The Impact of Planning and Goal Setting

A central theme throughout this guide has been the importance of setting clear goals and creating a plan to achieve them. This principle is the bedrock of success in any online income avenue. Whether you're launching an e-commerce store, starting a freelancing career, or entering the world of investments, having well-defined goals and a roadmap for reaching them is essential.

Recall the SMART framework for goal setting: Specific, Measurable, Achievable, Relevant, and Time-Bound. Break down long-term goals into smaller, achievable steps, and regularly track your progress. This systematic approach will keep you on the path to success.

The Significance of Financial Management and Tax Awareness

Proper financial management and a solid understanding of tax obligations are vital for sustained success in the online income world. Neglecting financial aspects can lead to financial instability and legal troubles.

Budgeting, separating business and personal finances, maintaining an emergency fund, saving, and investing are all key components of effective financial management. Being aware of your tax responsibilities, reporting income accurately, using deductions, and meeting tax payment deadlines are equally critical.

For more complex financial situations, consider seeking advice from a financial advisor or tax professional who can help you navigate these aspects of your online income journey.

The Motivation and Resilience to Succeed

Staying motivated and resilient is fundamental to achieving your online income goals. The digital world offers numerous opportunities, but it also presents challenges. Maintaining motivation and bouncing back from setbacks is an essential part of the journey.

Set milestones and celebrate small achievements along the way. Visualize your success, find a support system, take regular breaks to avoid burnout, and continue learning and growing in your field.

Adapt to changes, develop resilience to face adversity, establish a routine, cultivate a positive mindset, and maintain a long-term perspective. These principles will keep you motivated and persistent as you pursue your online income goals.

The Journey Ahead

This guide has provided a comprehensive overview of various methods to generate income online, from freelancing and e-commerce to investments, and offered tips for success in each of these avenues. It's important to recognize that your journey is unique, and there's no one-size-fits-all approach to online income generation.

As you proceed, consider the principles and insights shared throughout this guide. Use them as a foundation upon which to build your success. Adapt, learn, and persevere in the ever-evolving digital landscape.

Whether you aspire to become a successful freelance writer, launch a thriving online store, or build a diverse investment portfolio, the path to online income success is yours to navigate. The online world is dynamic, and it rewards those who are willing to learn, adapt, and persist.

Final Thoughts

In conclusion, online income generation is not just about financial gain. It's about personal growth, self-discovery, and the opportunity to pursue your passions and interests. It's about creating a lifestyle that aligns with your values and desires.

By taking the knowledge and principles shared in this guide and applying them to your unique journey, you have the potential to achieve remarkable success in the digital world. Whether you seek financial freedom, a flexible work-life balance, or the opportunity to make a meaningful impact, the online income avenues are vast and accommodating.

Your journey begins with a single step, and this guide has equipped you with the tools and insights to take that step with confidence. As you embark on your path to online income success, embrace the challenges, celebrate the victories, and never lose sight of your goals. The possibilities are endless, and your potential is boundless in the digital realm. Best of luck on your journey toward online income   success!

Chapter 10: Additional information and Places to Learn From

This chapter is like a treasure chest full of extra things, places to find information, and tools to help you as you learn about making money online. Doing well in the digital world often means learning a lot and being flexible. In this chapter, we give you a big list of stuff to help you stay informed, get better at things, and meet people who can help you make money online.

Where to Learn Online

1. **Coursera:** Coursera has many classes from good universities on things like business, technology, and starting your own business.

2. **edX:** Like Coursera, edX has classes from good universities, so you can learn new skills and get an education.

3. **Udemy:** Udemy has lots of classes on many things, like making websites or marketing, and they don't cost too much.

4. **LinkedIn Learning (used to be Lynda):** Now it's part of LinkedIn, and they have classes on business, technology, and creative skills.

5. **Khan Academy:** They have free stuff to learn about lots of different subjects, which is great if you like teaching yourself.

6. **Codecademy:** If you want to learn to code or get better at it, Codecademy is good for beginners and people who know a little already.

Where to Read and Watch

1. **Neil Patel:** Neil Patel writes and makes videos about online marketing and how to do it right.

2. **Smart Passive Income:** Pat Flynn writes a blog and makes a podcast about building businesses and making money without working all the time.

3. **Moz:** Moz is the place to go for info on SEO and digital marketing. They have a blog and guides that people in the business really like.

4. **Investopedia:** If you like money stuff and investing, Investopedia has articles, guides, and a dictionary for you.

5. **Copyblogger:** If you want to be good at content marketing and writing, Copyblogger is where you learn.

6. **TechCrunch:** Keep up with what's happening in the tech world, like new startups and cool gadgets, with TechCrunch's news and articles.

Where to Talk and Ask Questions

1. **Reddit:** Reddit has a lot of groups where you can talk about making money online, starting a business, and investing. Groups like r/Entrepreneur and r/investing are busy with people who want to help.

2. **Stack Overflow:** If you're a coder or programmer, Stack Overflow is where you ask questions and get help with coding.

3. **Indie Hackers:** Indie Hackers is a community of people who do their own thing in business, and they share stories and tips.

4. **Quora:** You can ask questions and talk to experts about all kinds of stuff, including business and tech, on Quora.

5. **Warrior Forum:** This place talks a lot about internet marketing and has discussions, reviews, and advice about making money online.

Tools and Programs

1. **Google Analytics:** This tool helps you see who comes to your website and what they do there. It's important for people doing business online.

2. **Mailchimp:** Lots of people use Mailchimp to send emails to their customers and build good relationships.

3. **Trello:** Trello is a tool that helps you keep track of your tasks and goals and is good for all kinds of projects.

4. **Hootsuite:** For managing social media and planning when to post things, Hootsuite is popular with marketers and social media stars.

5. **Canva:** Canva is a user-friendly tool for making good-looking pictures and stuff for your online projects.

6. **Mint:** Mint helps you keep track of your money, like what you make and spend and where you invest.

Books to Read

1. **"The Lean Startup" by Eric Ries:** This book teaches you how to start a business by being smart and not wasting time or money.

2. **"Rich Dad Poor Dad" by Robert Kiyosaki:** This classic book talks about money and investing and helps you make better decisions.

3. **"Crush It!" by Gary Vaynerchuk:** Find out how to build your personal brand and make money from your passion.

4. **"The 4-Hour Workweek" by Timothy Ferriss:** Learn how to make your life balance work and fun by thinking smart and living well.

5. "The $100 Startup" by Chris Guillebeau: This book gives you advice on starting a tiny business without spending much money.

1. Internal Revenue Service (IRS): If you're in the U.S., the IRS site has everything you need for taxes and online income.

2. Securities and Exchange Commission (SEC): The SEC website helps you understand the rules for investing and what you can and can't do.

3. Small Business Administration (SBA): If you're starting a small business online, the SBA can help with loans, advice, and support.

Places to Sell Stuff

1. Upwork: If you want to work for yourself, Upwork is where you find jobs and clients in different fields.

2. Fiverr: Fiverr is another place where you can offer your skills and services to people who need them.

3. **Amazon:** If you're thinking about selling stuff online, Amazon is a huge marketplace to do it.

4. **eBay:** eBay is famous for online auctions and selling all kinds of things.

5. **Etsy:** If you make cool stuff, you can sell it on Etsy, which is great for creative people.

10.8 Podcasts to Listen To

1. **"Smart Passive Income" by Pat Flynn:** Pat Flynn's podcast has tips on making money online and building businesses that run themselves.

2. **"Online Marketing Made Easy" by Amy Porterfield:** Amy Porterfield's podcast talks about digital marketing and making lists and online courses.

3. **"Indie Hackers" by Courtland Allen:** Indie Hackers interviews people who work for themselves and share their stories.

4. **"The Dave Ramsey Show" by Dave Ramsey:** Dave Ramsey talks about managing your money and investments.

5. "The Tim Ferriss Show" by Tim Ferriss: Tim Ferriss talks to really good people in all kinds of fields, and you can learn a lot from them.

Conferences and Big Events

1. **Web Summit:** It's one of the biggest tech conferences and covers lots of stuff about tech and business.

2. **SXSW (South by Southwest):** SXSW is a big event with music, movies, and tech, and it's good for people who like new ideas.

3. **FinCon:** If you make content about money, FinCon is a good place to meet people and learn stuff.

4. **eTail:** eTail is a conference for online stores and people who sell things on the internet.

5. **Collision:** This tech conference is all about tech, startups, and cool new things.

Places to Meet People and Join Groups

1. **Chambers of Commerce:** Local groups help businesses and people who work for themselves meet and learn from each other.

2. **Professional Associations:** Joining groups that match what you do can help you meet people and learn more. Like the American Marketing Association or the Freelancers Union.

Money News and Stuff to Read

1. **The Wall Street Journal:** It's a big source of business news and money info.

2. **Bloomberg:** Bloomberg talks about business and money from all over the world.

3. **Financial Times:** It looks at money, business, and economics from around the world.

4. **Forbes:** Forbes covers a lot about business, money, and starting your own business.

5. **The Motley Fool:** It's where people who care about the stock market get their news and advice.

Research and Reports

1. **Pew Research Center:** They study the internet and tech trends, which can help you make money online.

2. Statista: Statista has data, research, and reports about different industries and online money topics.

Places to Talk and Join

1. Facebook Groups: There are lots of groups on Facebook where freelancers, business owners, and people who work online talk. Find a group that's right for you and join in.

2. LinkedIn Groups: LinkedIn has groups where you can talk to people and learn about making money online and being an entrepreneur.

More Stuff to Read and Stories

Look for stories about people who made money online and read about them. Blogs and forums often have these stories and tips from people who did well.

Where to Get More Info

In this guide, you've seen lots of places to get info and read more. When you're looking into something specific, check out the sources we talked about to learn more.

Remember that doing well with online money is about learning and being ready for change. These places and info are your friends as you walk this road to online money success.   Good   luck   on   your   journey!